Advent Devotional:
the Jesse Tree

Discipleship Ministry Team
Ministry Council
Cumberland Presbyterian Church

October 2012

8207 Traditional Place
Cordova (Memphis), Tennessee 38016

The Discipleship Ministry Team of the Ministry Council of the Cumberland Presbyterian Church is the successor organization to the Board of Christian Education of the Cumberland Presbyterian Church.

Edited by Jodi Hearn Rush, cover and interior artwork by Jamie Price, cover design by Joanna Bellis.

Funded, in part, by your contributions to Our United Outreach.

First Edition: October 2012

Published by The Discipleship Ministry Team, CPC
Memphis, Tennessee

ISBN-13: 978-0615702735
ISBN-10: 0615702732

OUR UNITED OUTREACH
Made Possible In Part By Your Tithe To Our United Outreach

Advent Devotional: the Jesse Tree

Introduction

The Jesse Tree is an Advent custom that uses
symbols for Biblical characters for each day during
the Advent season. This tree is not just any tree - it is
the family tree of Jesus. In Isaiah 11:1 we read: *"A
shoot shall come out from the stump of Jesse,
and a branch shall grow out of his roots."* The
tree that grows with the symbols each day is a way in
which to tell the Biblical stories, bridge the Old and
New Testament stories together, and lead us through
the Advent season to the birth of Jesus Christ.

**You may use this book in a group, as a family, or as
an individual daily devotion. Either way, here are
some suggestions on how to use this book:**

♦ **Read the daily scripture** suggested at the
beginning of each devotion.

♦ **Look at the symbol** on the page to help you
recall the Bible story throughout the day and
throughout the Advent season.

♦ **Read the daily devotion** knowing that all of the
devotions were written by members of the
Cumberland Presbyterian Church and the
Cumberland Presbyterian Church in America
family - children, youth, and adults sharing
their stories as a gift to you this Advent season.

♦ **Pray the prayers** that are provided and add
your own prayers especially praying for the
writer of the devotion.

◆ **Use the Story Stretchers** at the end of each devotion to "stretch" the story and help you think about how the story relates to your life. If you are using this in a family or group setting, use this time to discuss unfamiliar words or ideas in the scripture or devotion.

◆ **Make a Jesse Tree.** A Jesse Tree can be as simple as a poster that you can add the daily symbols to, or as elaborate as a small tree decorated with the symbol ornaments for each day. Symbols to copy for use on a Jesse Tree are found at the back of this book. Or, you can make your own Jesse Tree ornaments from items you find around your church or home.

Advent Devotional: the Jesse Tree

December 1

The Family Tree
Matthew 1: 1 - 17

It seems an odd way to start such an beautiful and powerful Gospel, seventeen verses detailing a family genealogy from Abraham to Jesus. Placed at the very beginning of the New Testament, many people would point to the fact that Matthew's Gospel is a bridge of sorts from the Old Testament to the New Testament. You see, in order to get everyone's attention that Matthew was writing to, the Jewish people who were waiting for the Messiah to come, Matthew's opening genealogy would have been a powerful opening argument for those Jews desperate for their Redeemer. Somehow though, these verses have lost their power over time and many people will quickly pass over the names included to get to the *good stuff,* the miracles, the ministry, the parables, the passion and the resurrection.

During this season of Advent, we must challenge ourselves not to quickly pass over these verses from Matthew and to read them with the same anticipation and joy as the Jewish people of that day. They were excited because these seventeen verses told them they belonged, that they had a part to play in the Good News Matthew was about to give them. So, you are encouraged to read the seventeen verses slowly and carefully, and as you do recall the many stories you know about the people mentioned, and know that the *good stuff* to follow would not be possible without those who came before. Through this genealogy, we are given a small peek at God's plan, and yes, we belong to the plan - *now how exciting is that?*

Prayer: God, we thank you for the glimpses you give in unexpected places of your plans for us. We are thankful to realize that we are a part of those plans and we are thankful to know that we belong to you. *Amen*

– *Written by : Lisa Cook*

Story Stretchers

♦ Make a list of family members who came before you.

♦ Spend some time over the next few days looking at pictures of family members.

♦ Pick one of the people mentioned in today's scripture and find their "story" in the Bible.

Creation
Genesis 1: 26- 31

Do you know why the Creation story is important in our faith as Christians? Here are some reasons I feel the story of Creation is important.

First, it is the beginning of time and space. There are people who say that God didn't create the universe. They say that the universe was formed by an explosion. One can say or think, ***"Well, what if God wanted or caused the big explosion to happen?"*** Whichever way you believe, the fact remains that God did create the universe - and to me that is the bottom line.

Second, it shows God is all powerful. God created everything. God created all the birds of the air, the fish in the sea, and all creatures that move along the earth. Then God created the most wonderful thing of all.... us!

Without the creation of humans - humans would not have made mistakes and sinned - without sin Jesus would not have entered our world in a human form to teach us right from wrong - if Jesus did not come into the world to teach us, we would not have an Advent season to celebrate.

Prayer: Dear Lord, we praise you for all you have created this Advent season. ***Amen***

– Written by: Josh Tyler

Story Stretchers

♦   Think of one thing in creation that you really enjoy, and say a prayer of thanks for it today.

♦   Read both creation stories - in Genesis 1: 1 - 31 and Genesis 2: 4 - 23 - and compare how they are the same and how they are different.

December 3

Adam and Eve
Genesis 3: 1-7

The Adam and Eve story often ends with an, **"Oh, no!"** poor Adam and Eve were tricked by that snake and now they are in trouble. However, there is more to the story...

God created Adam, the first man, from the dust of the ground and breathed life into him. For a companion for Adam, God created Eve, the first woman, from one of Adam's ribs. They lived together happily in the Garden of Eden that God had planted for them. The garden had plants of all kinds growing with rivers flowing to water the garden. In the middle of the garden was the tree that gives knowledge of good and evil. It was this tree that God warned Adam not to eat from or he would die.

That sneaky snake tempted Eve by making the choice to eat from the forbidden tree, seem like a wise choice because she would gain knowledge. Adam, who was with Eve in the garden, also ate from the forbidden tree. It was this sin, committed by Adam and Eve that created the need for a savior.

After Adam and Eve were banished from the Garden of Eden as punishment for their sin, they started a family. The family tree of Adam and Eve includes their third son, Seth, Noah and Abraham, Isaac, and Jacob. The family tree also includes Jacob, Ruth, Jesse, and King David. Both Joseph and Mary's family tree include King David. *"For God so loved the world* (even sinners like Adam and Eve and you and me) *that God gave God's one and only Son* (whose earthly family tree began with Adam and Eve), *that whoever believes in God shall not perish but have eternal life."* John 3:16

Prayer: God, please help us to make good choices today. *Amen*

 - *Written by Stacey, Ava, and Jessi Bolin*

Story Stretchers

♦ Think of a bad choice you have made that you first thought was a good choice.

♦ Do you have any decisions to make today? If so, how will you make a good decision?

Noah
Genesis 6: 11-22, 9: 8-13

When we think about the story of Noah and the ark, we might think about the Sunday school story, complete with pictures of all the happy animals lining up in twos and Noah and his smiling family watching. But the story is not all happy. The animals were probably scared and resisted being put on the ark. I imagine Noah's family had some arguments over his building the ark when it wasn't even raining. But Noah persisted anyway. Scriptures don't tell us if Noah and God talked during the process of building the ark, or while people ridiculed him, but it does tell us that Noah was faithful through it all. Noah trusted God and kept his faith through all of the distractions, human feelings, and difficulties he likely encountered. He showed an unbelievable amount of courage and faith.

The story of Noah, reminds me of Slone, a special friend with whom I grew up. Slone was told she had brain and spinal cancer and has kept her faith and trusted God through all her health challenges. She has focused on a rainbow, which is God's promise to carry her through to the end of treatments, to the end of medical tests and doctor visits, to the end of being a part-time high school student, and to the end of cancer in her body. In the story of Noah, the rainbow is a sign to all humankind that God will not destroy the earth by flood and that God keeps God's promises. Slone's rainbow represents God's faithfulness to her through her many challenges as she fights to get healthy. If Noah can be faithful in his circumstance, and Slone can be faithful in hers, let us all be faithful as well, knowing that God will always be with us.

Prayer: God, help us to have the courage to do what you need us to do. *Amen*

– Written by: Allison Carr

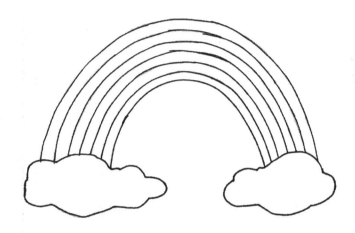

Story Stretchers

♦ Talk about a time when you or someone who you know has been courageous.

♦ As you go through the day, notice times when you or others act courageously.

December 5

Abram
Genesis 12: 1-7; Hebrews 11:8

When Abram was asked by God to leave everything behind and move to a new land, he did not know exactly what God was asking or **calling** him to do. He packed his belongings and moved his home - which in those days was not a house like we live in, but a tent. He didn't question God's request, he just followed God faithfully.

Today we may not hear the voice of God as Abram did, or as you hear a family member or a teacher's voice. But, we receive a call in the form of nudges, inspirations, or small voices inside our head. These callings from God may be asking you to do something that you may not feel able to do, or that does not seem to fit into your life or daily schedule. We are all encouraged to follow Abram's example, pick up our tents and following God's call, and we may just find the place that God wants us to pitch our tents.

I followed a nudge - *or a calling* - five years ago and that path has lead me to a place that I feel God meant for me to **pitch my tent**.

Prayer: God, lead us as you led Abram. Help us to follow your call with the same faith as Abram. ***Amen***

- Written by: Candy Barr

Story Stretchers

♦   Can you think of a time when you felt a nudge or small voice inside telling you to do something?

♦   Talk about how it might have been to live in a tent.

Jacob
Genesis 28: 10 - 22

As a young girl, I remember my Sunday school teacher, Sister Smith, who always had a knock-knock joke and a song for us to sing every Sunday in Sunday school. She began our class with *"Good morning children of the cross. How are you today?"* Then she would say. *"Knock-knock,"* and we would respond with *"Who's there?"* She would say, *"Jacob's ladder."* Then we would sing the song, **Jacob's Ladder.** With all my might, and the loudest voice - off key - I would sing:

We are climbing Jacob's ladder, We are climbing Jacob's ladder, We are climbing Jacob's ladder, Soldiers of the cross.

I did not like the song until later in life, but I now realize it is a story of how we can learn about God in many ways - even in our dreams.

Jacob's dream occurs at the end of perhaps the loneliest day of his life. Jacob had pulled off a scam, having stolen the birthright of his brother, Esau. He wrongly received the blessing from his father and was on the run for his life fearing his brother would kill him. Instead of a restful sleep which his exhausted body needed, Jacob had a dream in which he saw a ladder reaching from heaven to earth, with angels walking up and down, and God at the top. He saw a stairway made by God, and no matter who you are or what you have done, the stairway to God is always open to you.

Prayer: Lord, thank you for the promise that you will always be with us. ***Amen***

- Written by: Nancy Fuqua

Story Stretchers

♦ What do you think the *birthright in the story of Jacob and Esau means?

♦ Recall a time when you felt like you made a mistake. How did you feel?

*The birthright was usually given to the oldest son in the family. The one who received the birthright was honored with a double share of his father's inheritance. This was a special honor, for the birthright also included certain rights and privileges as well as responsibilities.

Joseph
Geneses 37: 1 - 4; 18 - 28; 45: 4-15

A quick summary of the story of Joseph would be: father showed favoritism, son showed arrogance, brothers showed jealousy, and the family was ripped apart by anger and bad decisions. In the center of the story was a coat. Although it was a fancy coat, it was just a coat. It was what the coat meant to each of the family members that caused it to become the reason for their sinful thoughts and actions.

For Jacob, the coat was a sign of his special love towards Joseph over his other sons. For Joseph, the coat was the symbol of his greatness and importance over his brothers. For the brothers, the coat was a reminder that they felt less important than their brother Joseph. All of these people were thinking bad thoughts, which led to bad decisions. It would be many years before the family saw how God made a blessing out of their bad thoughts and mistakes.

Prayer: God, help each of us to become a better family member, by putting away negative thoughts and replacing them with loving thoughts and actions toward our families. *Amen*

- Written by: By Paula Winn

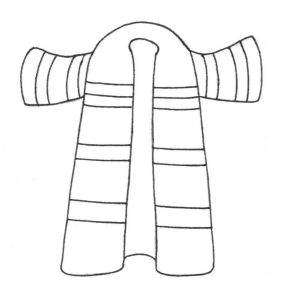

Story Stretchers

♦   Is there a "coat" or something like what happened in this story in your family that is causing unhappy thoughts and actions?

♦   What is something nice or helpful you can do for a family member today?

December 8

Moses
Exodus 3: 1 - 15

In the story of Moses and the burning bush, there is a great lesson to be learned about trusting and following God. Through his actions, Moses surrendered himself and learned to trust God to lead him down the path for his life. In our lives, we are placed in situations where we can choose to listen, follow, and trust God to lead us - or, we can go about our own way. Many times, we choose what we think may be the easier path and worry later about what God wants for our lives. We should try to live like Moses did by listening to God, surrendering ourselves, and realizing that God's plan is the best plan for our lives.

At one point in the story, God asks Moses to remove his sandals because he is standing on holy ground. We often find the idea of *holy ground* to be scary or something we don't understand. Most people view *holy ground* as something that happens only in a place of worship or something that happens to someone else. But really *holy ground* can be found everywhere, just like God is everywhere. *Holy ground* can happen for all people, not just for some people. *Holy ground* is a time or place where you feel God with you in a very real way. God creates these *holy ground moments* - or special moments where you feel God's presence - and God wants you to be present in these moments and to listen and to follow.

Growing up I can remember singing the hymn, **Standing on Holy Ground,** and wondering what on earth it meant. As I got older, I found my own burning bush in the words of the song:

In His presence I know there is joy beyond all measure,
and at His feet, sweet peace of mind can still be found.
For when we have a need, He is still the answer,
reach out and claim it for we are standing on holy ground.

Prayer: God, please help us to be prepared for *holy ground* moments. *Amen*

- Written by Abby Prevost

Story Stretchers

♦ In the devotion today the word ***surrender*** is used. What do you think that word means?

♦ The phrase holy ground is found twice in the Bible, once in the Old Testament story we read today and once in the New Testament in Acts 7:33. Look up the scriptures and read and compare the two holy ground scriptures.

♦ Have you ever been in a place that felt holy? Where was that and what was happening at the time?

Rahab
Joshua 2: 1 -14

Rahab is a woman of little worth in the eyes of her community, but God uses her in extra special ways. In the story we see this woman take two spies from a foreign land into her home and hide them from the rulers and authorities of her own country, Jericho. She knows these spies will be returning with troops to take over Jericho. More than that, she knows a more powerful God than anyone has ever known leads these two spies. Because she also believes in this God, she protects the spies from the king of Jericho and his men. In return, she asks the spies to protect her and her family when Jericho is invaded. The spies promise that if she ties a scarlet rope in her window she and her family will be protected.

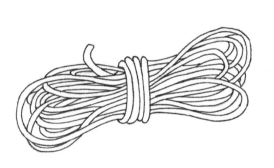

Rahab, a woman who people in her community didn't like, is not only an instrument for the nation of Israel to help them come into the land God had promised their ancestors long ago, but her story continues on centuries beyond her life. In Matthew 1:5 we see her name in a mighty list of characters that make up the family tree of Jesus Christ. She is the mother of Boaz.

She is the mother-in-law of Ruth. She is the great-great-grandmother of King David, who centuries later is an ancestor of Joseph, the husband of Mary, the parents of Jesus. If not for Rahab, the lineage from Abraham to Jesus would have been cut.

Prayer: God, we thank you for always being at work among us, even when we fail to see it. Remind us that your plans are perfect and reach further than our own. *Amen*

- *Written by: Whitney Brown*

Story Stretchers

♦ Can you think of someone that is an unlikely person serving God?

♦ Can you think of someone that others may not like and make a point to be their friend today?

♦ Have you ever done something brave like Rahab because you knew God would protect you?

Ruth
Ruth 1: 15 - 18; 2: 1-12

When Ruth married into the family of Elimelech, according to the customs of the time, she belonged to them. After the death of her husband, Ruth's mother-in-law, Naomi, released her from her obligation to the family. In Bethlehem, away from her own family and familiar customs, Ruth shows how she truly belongs to Naomi. As a result of Ruth's faithfulness and obedience, Naomi looks upon her as her own daughter and they stay in Bethlehem together. Elimelech's relative, Boaz, takes an interest in Ruth. Impressed by her faithfulness, he goes out of his way to make sure Ruth has enough to eat and a safe place to search for food.

In this part of the story, Naomi focuses upon the bad events of her life as if they were punishments from God rather than seeing Ruth's faithfulness as a gift. Ruth's devotion to Naomi is a blessing to the older woman. Boaz marries Ruth, and their child Obed will be the father of Jesse, the father of King David. From difficult times, God brings hope through those who are faithful. Ruth shows us that anyone may be adopted into

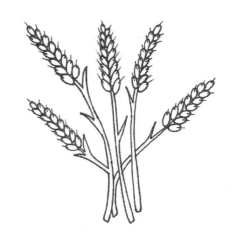

the kin-dom (kingdom) of God; it is not an exclusive lineage. From that adoption, God brings great things.

Prayer: God of grace, we ask you to bless our family by increasing our faithfulness to each other and to you. *Amen*

- Written by: Joy Warren

Story Stretchers

♦   What do you think it means to glean the fields as Ruth did in this story?

♦   Find a friend or family member and play a game of *Follow the Leader* to remember Ruth's faithfulness in following and staying with Naomi.

♦   There are many different kinds of families as we read about in today's scripture. Draw a picture of your family.

Jesse
Isaiah 11: 1 - 2

A shoot of new life coming from a dead tree stump gives us a description of the anticipated new beginning of the Jewish people after they had to leave their country and were ruled by strangers, and a promise that one of David's descendants would come to the throne. We read from the prophets some of the qualities the Messiah will have - a role that only Jesus could fill.

With the birth of Jesus, it was as if new life came from a stump of a tree that had been cut down and left to die. Though some thought that it was dead, the roots of the stump remained alive and they grew a branch. This Advent season we celebrate the birth of one who was filled with wisdom, understanding, good counsel, power and might, and knowledge of God.

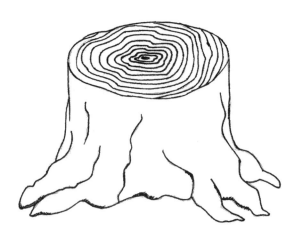

Prayer: Glory be to the most high God who is able to bring life from any situation. Thank you for the birth of a Savior to die for our many sins. Continue to remind us of your life even when the world shows us otherwise. *Amen*

 - *Written by: Abby* Rogers

Story Stretchers

♦   Look at this stump in the picture, or find one out in nature. Does it look like life could come from the stump?

♦   What do you think the word *Messiah* means?

* The title Messiah was used by the people and the prophets to refer to the leader that they were hoping and waiting for. This leader, or great king, would deliver them and rule over the world.

December 12

Samuel
1 Samuel 3: 1 - 20

In this passage, Samuel keeps hearing his name and he thinks it's Eli, the temple priest, calling him. Every time he said to Eli, *"Here I am. Did you call me?"* Eli always said, *"I didn't call you."* Then the last time Eli said to Samuel *"Say, 'Speak Lord your servant is listening."* Samuel didn't know about God because he hadn't heard God's voice yet. Samuel served the Lord by working for Eli. Eli needed help because he was almost blind. Eli helped Samuel know about God and become a servant of God.

When Jesus came He helped us know more about God. Jesus helped us know God by talking to us and by loving us. God sent Jesus because God loves us. Jesus was born and died to help us know God.

I have people who help me know about God. My mom and dad help me know God by reading the Bible and praying. Mrs. Barbara Sutton, my Sunday school teacher, helps me know God by helping me know about stories from the Bible. This Advent season, how will you help others know about God?

Prayer: God, thank you for loving us so much. Help us do good things and love others no matter what. *Amen*

- Written by: Victoria Hassell

Story Stretchers

♦   Think about a person who has helped you to know about God, and say a prayer of thanks for them today.

♦   The symbol for today's story is a lamp. Sometimes we need a lamp to see where we are going. Besides a lamp or other light source, what can we use to "see" or understand something that is unclear to us?

December 13

David
1 Samuel 16: 1 - 13

In today's daily scripture reading, we read about David, the youngest son of Jesse, and Samuel, who God asked to travel to Bethlehem to anoint a new king. After Jesse presents all of his sons to Samuel, except David, Samuel tells Jesse that none of these sons are the one that the Lord wants to choose. Jesse's youngest son, David is summoned from the field where he is taking care of the sheep. David was the last of his sons that Jesse thought the Lord would want to pick. When David arrives, the Lord told Samuel to take the horn of oil and anoint David. David went on to become a great king.

This story is a great example of how we incorrectly judge God's design and how different our thoughts are from God's. Jesse thought God would want a stronger, older son, but God wanted the youngest of the group, the one who had been watching over the sheep. Through his work as shepherd, and his protecting of the flock, he was being prepared to watch over the people one day as king.

During this Advent season, let us follow the lessons learned in this scripture, no matter how unprepared or unworthy you may feel, God can and will use you, to glorify God's kingdom.

Prayer: God, help us not to look at the outward appearance of people we meet. Help us look at their hearts. *Amen*

- Written by: Kile Garrett

Story Stretchers

♦ What are some of the jobs a shepherd must do to take care of the sheep?

♦ How does it feel to be chosen for something? How do you think David felt being chosen for anointing by Samuel?

♦ What do you think it meant when Samuel used a horn of oil to anoint David?

Solomon
1 Kings 3: 3 - 15

Recently, I attended a pastor's anniversary program in which the congregation was presenting gifts to their pastor. One family after another presented a gift to the pastor. A woman stood up with her eyes full of tears and expressed her thankfulness and appreciation for the pastor's support and encouragement during her life when times had been difficult. She spoke of how her husband had left her and her two children and how she lost her job all in the same year. She then told the pastor that she had no money to buy him a gift to express her gratitude, so instead her gift to him would be a spiritual praise dance. In the middle of the song the woman's children both stood up and started to dance along with their mother, missing a step here and there. The children were unsure of the next move, but they stayed with the routine as they looked up at their mother for guidance. The gift, given by this family, was not like any of the other gifts - but, it was an important gift for the pastor to receive.

Solomon, King David's son, loved the Lord. God came to Solomon in a dream and asked him, ***"What shall I give you?"*** Solomon told God that he was not sure how to lead and be a good leader for the people. Instead of asking for riches - as might have been expected - Solomon asked God to give him an understanding mind as he led the people. This request pleased God because Solomon did not ask for things that benefitted him but that benefitted others.

Prayer: God, in the middle of a season where we will be receiving many gifts, help us to ask you for wisdom and understanding as Solomon did. ***Amen***

-Written by: Darius Holden

Story Stretchers

♦ What is something you need wisdom or understanding about?

♦ During this Advent season, how can we put others before ourselves?

♦ Today's symbol is a picture of the Ark of the Covenant, a beautiful box used to hold the two stones with the Ten Commandments written on them. The Israelites carried the Ark throughout their wanderings in the desert and eventually Solomon placed the Ark in the temple. This was a symbol to the people of God's presence with them. What are symbols of God's presence with you in your home or church?

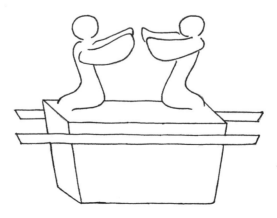

Josiah
2 Kings 22: 1-13 & 23: 1 - 3

Josiah became king at age eight. He had to assume a big responsibility. He had to accomplish the daily duties of being a king as well as doing what was right in the eyes of the Lord. It must have been particularly hard since Josiah's father had not served God well. He didn't have an earthly example to follow. In spite of this disadvantage, he was determined to be a good king and follow God.

When Josiah served eighteen years, he sent money for the temple to be repaired. During the repairs, a book of God's laws was discovered and was taken to King Josiah. When Josiah heard the words of the book he tore his robes from his body because he was so upset that all the laws were not being followed. Even though he had tried to be a good king and lead the people in God's ways, he had not had a copy of the law and had not known all of God's law.

Can you think of a time when you have been given a lot of responsibility in a leadership role, and it was tough to make the right choices? In the Bible story, when everyone was disobeying the law and doing wrong in the eyes of the Lord, Josiah continued doing the right thing, not only when everyone was watching him, but also in everything he did. When we find ourselves in situations too big to handle on our own and are tempted to give up or make bad choices, we don't have to *"tear our robes"* like Josiah did. Instead we can pray to God for help. Just like God helped Josiah, God will help you do what is right.

Prayer: God, when our responsibilities and our choices are too big to handle on our own, remind us to come to you in prayer. *Amen*

-Written by: Jonathan Bellis

Story Stretchers

♦ How do you think it would feel to be king at age eight?

♦ Instead of *"tearing your robe"* what is something you do when you are frustrated or upset?

December 16

Isaiah
Isaiah 2:4; 7:14; 9: 6-7

"Immanuel" - literally means **God with us.** A prophecy
was fulfilled by Jesus Christ roughly 2,000 years ago.
Advent is always an exciting time of the year. There is the
hustle and bustle of shopping and preparing for
Christmas. But, the season of Advent also brings to mind
the peaceful thoughts of snow falling, carolers going from
house to house, and the warmth of friends and family.
Yet, this peace is only temporary. The verses in Isaiah,
tell of a hope of lasting peace, peace that is brought by the
promise of God, peace that is brought through Immanuel -
God with us.

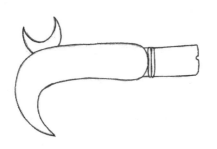

In our scripture
today, it is said
that swords will be
changed into plows,
and spears into
pruning hooks. A
pruning hook is a
tool used for cutting
back trees that have gotten too big to be useful.
Sometimes we need to go through a type of **pruning** to
get rid of things in our life that are not helpful. The more
of these things that are pruned, the more like Jesus we
will be.

Prayer: Thank you for the hope of lasting peace that comes through Immanuel. *Amen*

- Written by: Jeff and Stacy DeWees

Story Stretchers

♦ If you had a pruning hook for parts of your life that are not like God would want them to be - what would you *prune* or get rid of?

♦ In the devotion you read the word - **prophecy.* What do you think this word means?

♦ "Immanuel" means God with us. How do you feel God is with you today?

* Prophecies are statements made about future events.

December 17

Jeremiah
Jeremiah 23: 5-6; 31: 31-34

Most of us have probably heard the word **covenant** before. But, do we know what it truly means? A covenant is a mutual agreement between parties. In the scripture passage for today we are told of a king who will come in the future and will save Judah and Israel. This king is of course, Jesus. We then learn that the Lord will make a new covenant with Israel and Judah. It is a brand new covenant, unlike the one that the Lord made with the ancestors of the current peoples of Israel and Judah.

Today's symbol is a heart. When most individuals think of a heart, they think of love. In the scripture for today, God shows love and mercy towards the peoples of Israel and Judah. Although the ancestors messed up and God could have easily decided to not make a new covenant. God does make the covenant because God loves them and is a God of mercy. This covenant is important in the time leading up to Jesus' birth because it shows what kind of king he will be; one of mercy and love. When you think of a heart today, remember that God loves us all and is merciful upon you every day of your life.

Prayer: Lord, today, please help us to remember how much you love us and the kindness you show us. ***Amen***

- Written by: Michael Laperche Jr.

Story Stretchers

♦ Jeremiah was a *prophet. What do you think it means to be a prophet? How do you think it would feel to be a prophet when people did not listen to you?

♦ Words of hope can be found all through the book of Jeremiah. What is something you hope for?

♦ Think of someone who is sad or hurting today - ***someone in need of hope.*** Make a card with a heart on it to give to them to remind them of that hope.

* A prophet is a person who tells God's message to others.

December 18

Daniel
Daniel 6: 1 - 23

This Advent season we have the chance to kneel in prayer as Daniel did in our scripture today. Daniel openly knelt in prayer before God even though life threatening laws said he wasn't suppose to. The people Daniel worked with hated him because he was Jewish. They did not want him to be their leader. In order to stop this from happening they plotted against him. They got him in trouble by using his devotion to God to put him in conflict with the law. They proposed a law that all people should pray only to the king. It was an unfair law because its purpose was to hurt a specific group of people, not to be helpful for all.

Unfair laws are written all around the world. We probably know some of God's people that are being affected by them. For example, some children are deeply hurt by unfair laws about immigration. When the law is enforced, their parents go to jail and the children are separated from their parents and go to foster homes. They are treated as criminals without having broken a law. Our responsibility to such unfairness is to pledge our allegiance to Christ's kingdom more than to any other earthly power.

It did not matter that Daniel's life was in danger, he decided to openly kneel in prayer three times a day as he had been used accustomed to doing. He did not hide his devotion to God. He publically prayed even though he faced death for doing this.

Prayer: Jesus Christ, deliver us from unfair laws as we humbly kneel to pray to you. *Amen*

- Written by: Rev. Gloria and Rev. Fredy Diaz & Benjamin

Story Stretchers

♦ Do you ever kneel when you pray? Why don't you try it today?

♦ Do you know of any rules or laws that you think are unfair?

♦ Have you ever witnessed someone being treated unfairly?

Jonah
Jonah 1 - 4

At some point in your life, God will want you to do something, and all you will want to do is run away from it. Recently, I have discovered that God's plan for my life is for me to become a missionary. In order for me to realize this, God had to shake me up and get my attention so that I would listen to what God was calling me to do with my life. Not all of us are called to go to other countries and share God's word, but you might be called to witness to that person who is intimidating at work or school. You may be called to be friends with a person that nobody really likes. You may be called to forgive someone who has done something to you that you feel is unforgivable.

Jonah was willing to tell the Ninevites about the destruction they would face if they did not repent or change the way they were living, but he was unwilling to forgive them for their past sins. God, however, was so happy that they were changing their ways, that God accepted them with the same open arms that are offered to each one of us. God is a God of forgiveness and compassion, so we should also be people of forgiveness and compassion.

Whatever God wants you to do, you should do, even if it means answering God's call to be a full-time or short-term missionary, becoming friends with an unlikely person, or forgiving another person.

Prayer: God, help me to obey and listen to the call you have for our lives. ***Amen***

-Written by: Whitney Bond

Story Stretchers

♦ Think of a time when it was really hard to what was right?

♦ What do you think it means to be called by God?

♦ What type of work do you think a missionary is called to do?

♦ What do you think God is calling you to do for someone else today?

December 20

Zechariah
Luke 1: 5 - 23

A man of God named Zechariah,
was a burner of incense, hence no pariah,
when startled by the angel at the right of the altar
at the promise of a son found he had to falter.

Gabriel apparently had become tired
of elderly humans disbelieving they've sired,
and for Zechariah's failure in the class of aplomb
the angel of God blithely struck him dumb.

Elizabeth, on the other hand, did not think it odd,
and bypassing her husband, gave credit to God.
The lesson is clear, with no if, and, or but,
in the presence of angels, best keep your mouth shut.

Prayer: God, in this season of gratefulness, remind of the lesson of Zechariah, and let all our expressions be ones of gratitude, and not of doubt. *Amen*

 - Written by: David Dean

Story Stretchers

♦   When Zechariah was in the sanctuary, an angel appeared to him. The angel said, *"Do not be afraid."* Do you know another person in the New Testament that this angel appeared to and said these same words? You can read about this in Luke 1:30.

♦   Zechariah was so surprised by the news the angel gave him, he questioned the angel. Can you recall a time when you received news that was so surprising you asked many questions?

♦   Reread the poem with the Advent devotional in one hand and the Bible in the other. Go through line by line and match the lines of the poem with the verses of scripture.

December 21

Elizabeth
Luke 1: 39 - 45, 57 - 60

Elizabeth and Zechariah had wanted children for quite some time. They had prayed to God asking God to bless them with the birth of a child. Elizabeth was growing older and had almost given up hope.

My husband and I were blessed with the birth of a baby boy in 2002. We had wanted more children but as we began to grow older and our son began to grow older, we realized this was not in our plans. God had another plan for us. When our oldest child was eight years old, we found out that we were going to be blessed with another child. Since we were not supposed to be able to have more children this was a complete shock to us. In 2010, God's gift of a healthy little girl was given to us.

Like Elizabeth, we had almost given up hope of having more children. Through the birth of our sweet little girl, we were reminded of the importance of patience, and waiting for something to happen. We must trust and obey, because God is in control and knows what we need and when we need it.

Prayer: God, thank you for teaching us patience. Help us to trust and obey You the same way that Elizabeth did. *Amen*

 - Written by: Mandy Clark

Story Stretchers

♦   Elizabeth had to wait a long time for her first child. When is a time you had to wait for something?

♦   In the scripture today, Mary travels to see Elizabeth. When are you traveling to see friends or family in the days ahead? Or, are others traveling to visit with you? How will you greet them when you see them for the first time?

♦   Our symbol today is of friends talking to each other to remind us of the time Mary and Elizabeth spent talking and sharing news with each other. What is some news you would like to share with a family member or a friend today?

John the Baptist
Mark 1: 1 - 8

People are announced to everyone in a lot of different
ways. Judges are announced before they enter the
courtroom by a deputy. Grand Marshals of parades are
usually announced at the start of the parade with police
cars who have their sirens blaring. Presidents are
announced before
they enter the
chamber. And, kings
and queens are
announced by herald
trumpeters. Jesus,
however, was
announced to the
people by John the
Baptist.

John the Baptist was totally unlike herald trumpeters.
But he was the one to announce the coming of Jesus. He
was dressed in camel's hair and a leather belt around his
waist. John understood who Jesus was, because he was
part of Jesus' family tree. Their mothers were cousins, so
they were cousins.

People were ready for the Messiah to come. It had been
written in the Old Testament book of Isaiah. John the
Baptist preached to prepare the people for Jesus. He
helped people understand God's message. Now, in this
Advent season, let's prepare ourselves for Jesus.

Prayer: Dear God, help us to be messengers by sharing Jesus with others. *Amen*

- Written by: Debbie Hayes

Story Stretchers

♦ How are you preparing for the celebration of the coming birth of Jesus?

♦ How can you be like John and spread the word about Jesus?

♦ John the Baptist baptized many people. Today's symbol is a shell, sometimes used for baptism. A minister might use a shell to pour water on the head of a person receiving baptism. What can you recall about your baptism? If you were too young to remember, ask someone who was present to tell you about your baptism.

Joseph of Nazareth
Matthew 1: 18 - 25

Every Christmas, we read about the prayer by Mary, the story of baby Jesus, and the joyful celebration of all the angels and shepherds. What about Joseph, the father of baby Jesus? Joseph was silent through the whole story. When I browse through the Gospels, Joseph didn't say a single word. He listens and obeys. Although we don't have any words that he said , we can still imagine the conversations he had with Mary, and the angel. We can **"hear"** him talking to the innkeeper. We can visualize him putting Mary and baby Jesus on a donkey to ride on their journey.

In today's scripture, Joseph probably thought his life was pretty well planned. His marriage and his future were all arranged neatly for him, but then his world came crashing down. When he found out Mary was pregnant, and not by him, he was disappointed. Joseph was a good and honest man. At first, he wanted to quietly divorce Mary and send her away secretly. After the Angel spoke to Joseph, he risked being questioned about Mary's pregnancy and married her.

Although Joseph came from the royal lineage of King David, we can picture him as a humble, quiet, hard working man. He accepted the circumstances surrounding Jesus' birth. He had faith that God would provide every step of the way. He didn't have any parenting books or any training on how to be a father to the Son of God, but he had faith and compassion. What more can you ask of any father?

Prayer: Loving God, teach us to be humble, obedient and have faith in you to provide for us every step of our way. ***Amen***

- Written by: Janet Sun

Story Stretchers

♦ Joseph was a carpenter and used many tools in his work. Who is someone that you know who works with tools?

♦ If you knew how to use tools, what is something you would like to make?

♦ Some of the words used to describe Joseph in today's devotional were: hard working, compassionate, humble, honest, and faithful. Who is someone that you know that has some of these traits that Joseph had?

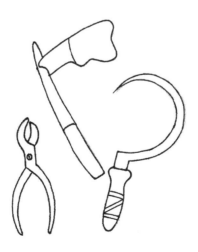

Mary
Luke 1: 26 - 38

I don't think I ever fully appreciated the story of Mary until I had a son of my own. Last Advent, while the church waited for the coming of Jesus, I was waiting on my first child, as well. By the time Christmas came around, I was eight and a half months pregnant. My excitement turned to impatience as my stomach expanded and my energy was gone. I remember wondering if the Savior of the world had caused His mother so many sleepless, uncomfortable nights.

When I read the first chapter of Luke, I cannot help but be filled with anxiety for poor Mary. It's one thing to enter into a loving relationship and willingly decide to have a child. It's quite another to be told, without any choice, that you will give birth to the Son of God. If I were Mary, I think I would have felt like asking if God was sure I was the right girl for the job! However, Mary didn't do that when she was called to be the vessel for God's saving grace. She was unsure of the how she would do what she was asked to do, but she said yes to God's plan.

Mary probably didn't know exactly how things would work out for her son. She probably never dreamed He would perform miracles or turn the world upside down. She probably never imagined that His death would cancel sin's stronghold on the world. Only God could imagine such a future for a tiny baby born to a faithful woman.

Prayer: Loving God , help us have faith like Mary's, So that when you call upon us, we might commit our whole selves to your purpose. *Amen*

- Written by: Chloe Duncan

Story Stretchers

♦ Have you ever been asked to do something and were not sure you could do what had been asked of you?

♦ With one more day in our Advent devotional, who has been your favorite Bible person to learn about? Why?

♦ In what ways can you continue to learn about these stories from the Bible?

December 25

Jesus
Luke 2: 1- 20

Today our daily devotion is about the baby Jesus. He was
born in a town called
Bethlehem inside a
stable. But before
that, an angel from
above told some
shepherds to spread
the joyful news! So the
shepherds did as the
angel said to do.

This story reminds me
of my sister's birth in 2006. My family and I spread the
joyful news of her birth just like the shepherds did when
Jesus was born. That's how this Bible story relates to me.
But how does this work for you? We should always talk
about Jesus and spread the great, wonderful, magnificent
word of God. I encourage you!

Prayer: Dear God, thank you for creating Jesus, because if
it wasn't for you, Jesus would not have died for our sins.
And, thank you for creating Mary and Joseph. In your
name we pray. *Amen*

- Written by: Jonathan Rice

Story Stretchers

♦ How does this work for you? How will you spread
the good news that Jesus is born?

Meet the Team

Authors:

Candy Barr is a member of First Cumberland Presbyterian Church in Rogersville, Alabama, where she serves as Preschool Director and Christian Education Director for children K-6. She is married to David Barr, and has two sons, Christopher and Daniel, a daughter- in- law, Janie, and a grandson, Apollo.

Jonathan Bellis is a member of the Orange Cumberland Presbyterian Church and is a Senior at Aurora High School in Aurora, Missouri. He serves as FFA chapter President, the Area 7 FFA President and Student Body President. Jonathan qualified to attend the World Livestock Judging competition in Scotland and won the World Champion Sheep contest. He raises Hereford cattle, plays the trombone in high school marching band, and helps lead praise songs at church.

Stacey Bolin is a member of Covenant Cumberland Presbyterian Church in Ada, Oklahoma, where she serves as Youth Director. She is a professor at East Central University and mom to two wonderful daughters, Ava and Jessi, who are 8 and 5. Ava enjoys reading and music. Jessi's favorite activity is art.

Whitney Bond attends Shiloh Cumberland Presbyterian Church in Ovilla, Texas. She is a member of the youth group and she recently went on a mission trip to Tanzania. Whitney plans to pursue a career as a medical missionary to Africa.

Whitney Brown is a member of Beaver Creek Cumberland Presbyterian Church, in Knoxville, Tennessee. She serves as the Presbyterial Youth and Children's Coordinator for the Presbytery of East Tennessee.

Allison Carr is a junior at Springfield Catholic High School. She attends White Oak Pond Cumberland Presbyterian Church in Lebanon, Missouri. Allison is a competitive swimmer on Springfield Aquatics in Springfield, Missouri. She serves the church by being a member of the planning council for the Cumberland Presbyterian Youth Conference, and a member of the Production Team for Presbyterian Youth Triennium.

Mandy Ellis Clark is a member of the Beersheba Cumberland Presbyterian Church in Columbus, Mississippi, where she serves as Children's Ministry Director. She is the Instructional Specialist for Pre-K - 5th grades at Franklin Academy. She enjoys being a Child of God, Daughter, Sister, Wife, Aunt, Mother, and Teacher.

Lisa Cook lives in Nashville, Tennessee, and has been a member of Brenthaven Church since 2007, where she teaches Sunday school. Lisa is a graduate of Bethel University and a current student of Memphis Theological Seminary where she is earning her Masters of Divinity degree in preparation for ordination in the Cumberland Presbyterian Church.

Jeff and Stacy DeWees live in the small community of Ramar, Tennessee, where Jeff serves as the stated supply pastor of Mt. Vernon Cumberland Presbyterian Church. They enjoy their family of four who enjoys running and spending time together.

David Dean is a member of Marshall Cumberland Presbyterian Church in Marshall, Texas, where he teaches Sunday school. He is a Battalion Chief in the Marshall Fire Department.

Rev. Gloria and Rev. Fredy Diaz are ordained Cumberland Presbyterian ministers and their son **Benjamin** (age 12) attend First Cumberland Presbyterian Church in Houston, Texas. Ben is an active musician. Gloria and Fredy have been working with multi-cultural ministries for about six years. Gloria's ministry focus is with inmates and their families, with Freddy's being with Latino families.

Chloe Lively Duncan lives in Huntsville, Alabama, with her husband, Matt, and son, Everett. She is a member of Christ Presbyterian Church of Monrovia.

Dr. Nancy J. Fuqua lives in Town Creek, Alabama, with her husband of 40 years, Cleoney. They have three sons, two daughter-in-laws, and six grandchildren. Nancy is the founding and Senior pastor of the New Life Cumberland Presbyterian Church in America, in Town Creek.

Kile Garrett is a student at Mars Hill College in North Carolina where he serves as the Student body Vice-President, an officer with Fellowship of Christian Athletes, and plays on the Lacrosse Team. When at home in Nashville, Tennessee, he attends Brenthaven Cumberland Presbyterian Church.

Victoria Hassell is a member of the Sturgis Cumberland Presbyterian Church in Sturgis, Kentucky. She is in the 6th grade at Union County Middle School. She loves music and playing piano.

Debbie Hayes is a member of Unity Cumberland Presbyterian Church, in Hardin, Kentucky, and is married to Rev. Brian Hayes. She is the Preschool Kindergarten Sunday school teacher, member of Cumberland Presbyterian Women's Ministry and in the church choir at Unity. She and Brian have two children, Brandon, a freshman at Bethel University and Kelsey a freshman in high school.

Darius Holden is a minister ordained by Huntsville Presbytery and serves at the Triana Cumberland Presbyterian Church in America. He attends Huntsville Bible College.

Michael Laperche Jr. attends Christ Cumberland Presbyterian Church in Florida. He is a senior in high school and lives just outside Tampa, Florida.

Abby Prevost is a member of First Cumberland Presbyterian Church in Columbus, Mississippi. She is a graduate of Bethel University. Through the Center for Youth Ministry Training program she is working on her next degree and serving as youth director at Flat Lick Cumberland Presbyterian Church in Kentucky.

Jonathan Perryn Rice is ten years old. He is a member of the First Cumberland Presbyterian Church in Cookeville, Tennessee, where he is very active in the children's ministry and choir. Jonathan has an orange belt in karate and placed second in the Smokey Mountain Christian Martial Arts Tournament in sparring for his age group. He enjoys reading funny books, playing video games, and working with computers. Jonathan lives with his parents, Perryn and Terri, and younger sister, Lauren Endia.

Abby Rogers or Reverend A'Yonnika Rogers is the Associate Minister at New Hope Cumberland Presbyterian Church in America. She attends Vanderbilt University in Nashville, Tennessee, and plans to pursue a Masters in Divinity and Counseling.

Janet Sun is an administrator at the Cumberland Presbyterian Chinese Church in San Francisco, California.

Josh Tyler attends First Cumberland Presbyterian Church in Dyersburg, Tennessee, where he is an active member of the youth group and also in the Youth Revolution choir. Josh attends Dyer County High School and plays the saxophone in the Dyer County Sound of the Choctaws Band.

Joy Warren is a Licentiate under the care of Nashville Presbytery. She will soon complete her Master of Divinity degree at Memphis Theological Seminary. Joy and her family live north of Nashville in Greenbrier, Tennessee, and attend Mt. Sharon Cumberland

Presbyterian Church.

Paula Winn grew up in Nashville Presbytery, claiming several churches as her church family. In particular, St. Luke, Clarksville, Mt. Liberty, and Dickson. For 15 years, she has co-directed Nashville Presbytery Junior Camp with one of her best friends, Jimmy Sharpe. Paula now lives in Sunbright, Tennessee, where she is active at First Cumberland Presbyterian of Oak Ridge.

Illustrators:

Joanna Bellis is originally from rural southwest Missouri where she grew up attending the Orange Cumberland Presbyterian Church. She has a degree in Commercial Art Graphic Design. Joanna now lives in Nashville where she is enrolled in the Center for Youth Ministry Training program, with only one year left to finish her Masters in Religion through Memphis Theological Seminary. Joanna works as the youth director at Brenthaven Cumberland Presbyterian Church, in Brentwood, Tennessee.

Jamie Price is from Germantown, Tennessee, and attended Germantown Cumberland Presbyterian Church. Jamie attended University of Tennessee at Martin where she played four years of soccer and earned a chemistry degree. She is currently a student at the University of Tennessee College of Pharmacy. Jamie loves running, dancing, and making memories with family and friends.

Family Tree

Creation

Adam and Eve

Noah

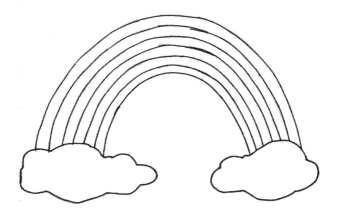

Abram

Jacob

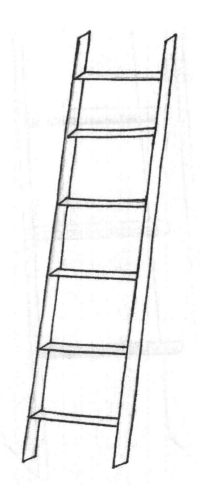

Joseph

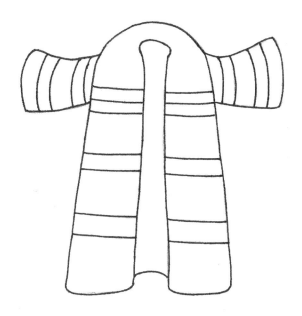

Moses

Rahab

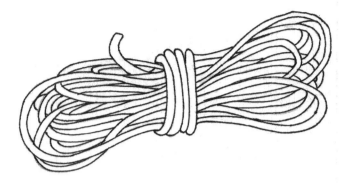

Ruth

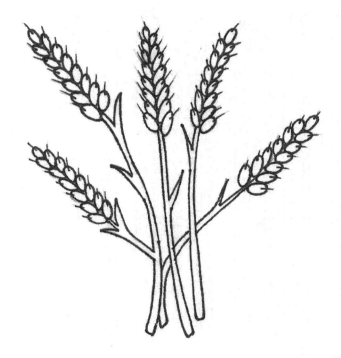

Jesse

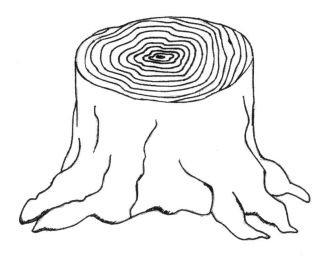

Samuel

David

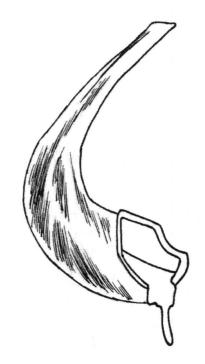

Solomon

Josiah

Isaiah

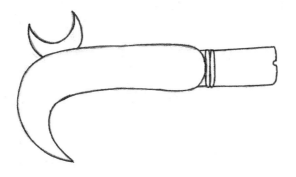

Jeremiah

Daniel

Jonah

Zachariah

Elizabeth

John the Baptist

Joseph

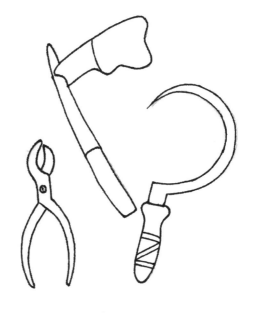

Mary

Jesus

Printed in Great Britain
by Amazon.co.uk, Ltd.,
Marston Gate.